Red Fox Run

Discovering Meaning in the
Poems We Write

Poems from a Poets' Retreat,
Murphy, North Carolina, October 19, 2013

GENE HIRSCH
Guide

RIDGELINE LITERARY ALLIANCE
www.ridgelineliterary.org

Rights revert to the individual poets on publication

Published by Ridgeline Literary Alliance
Hayesville, North Carolina, USA

ISBN 978-0615926926

CONTENTS

INTRODUCTION

I'd like you to meet some poets who came together for a one-day retreat. We were interested in exploring the issue of *meaning* in our poetry.

It has been said that without life there is no meaning and without meaning there is no life. Poets are in a unique position to understand this phrase in that we work hard in dealing with the meaning that flows beneath the words we write.

The word "meaning" has many usages such as intention (what are you intending to do), query (what do you mean), exclamation (what is the meaning of this), etc. Our use of the word speaks of personal value that opens up a discussion about a whole area of experience, thought, and feeling—for instance, *it has meaning for me because...* or *in this way...* or *it makes me feel..., or think..., or wonder...*

At our retreat, each of us read our poems and discussed their meanings for the poet and for each of the other participants. We discussed the *discovery and expression* of meaning. This proved to be a rich enterprise. It made us aware of five factors that may be obvious and intuitive, but that are frequently taken for granted:

- Meaning is found in what we *hold dear*. What we hold dear has *meaning*.

- Meaning comes to light as we discover the *essence* of what we are writing about. *Essence* is the intrinsic nature or indispensable quality of something that determines its character. For instance, the essence of this orange is in its wonderful flavor. This discovery frequently excites a *Eureka* experience.

- Discovering meaning implies assigning *value (holding dear)* something beyond what we have otherwise thought of as being merely significant or outstanding.

- Meaning can inspire a poem. It can appear to us as a poem unfolds for the poet, or later, when she reflects upon it. The poem formulates a meaning for the poet, one that she has subconsciously held, one that arises during the crafting or afterwards, on reflection of the poem. It is at these times that a poet learns most about herself and her life-worlds (what she gives to and receives from her personal environment). This is occasion for another *Eureka* experience, but at a deeper level.

• Meaning is the meeting place between the poet and the reader, as the reader contributes her own personal meaning to what she reads. In this way, they both come to *own and share feelings* about an essence—a third *Eureka* experience.

We invite you to read our poems (even aloud) more than once, with meaning in mind, to become aware of what each poem is trying to say for the poet and you. Do not be surprised if some words do not appear to make literal sense. It is the feeling that they impart that is important.

Red Fox Run was our meeting place, on a mountain in the woods. It was restful.

Gene Hirsch
Guide

Red Fox Run

The Poems

JOAN M. HOWARD

Eighty-Four Years Harvest

Monique's life springs now in the garden.
She counts camellias on a stem,
shares young snow peas as treasure,
bright lemons, grapefruit, jacaranda,
trades potatoes for rich ash,
builds hunting perches for bluebirds
knows the radius of their sight.

Hiding in a forest of larkspur
her cat Lili jumps up at bees.
She paints stones as ladybugs;
mirrors cut into butterflies
backed with sparkling paper
spin golden prisms in the wind.
Orchids are her greatest luxury.

Monique spends evenings on the phone
with cultivated companions
laughing, long breathless descriptions
of orioles, new wood ducks nesting,
nine inch growth of a rose cutting,
dawn waterings, sun, radiate joy.

The First Moment

Fifty years ago
my first glance
casually sent
no obstructions:
your body profiled
quietly intact
seated...
curling brown hair
arm resting on the desk
foot uplifted on the bottom rungs;

both of us waiting
both of us completely unaware.

What precision,
from where
that golden arrow?

Southern Summer

Southern wet drenched sun
quaking the afternoon,
vibrations so intense
we carefully, slowly crawl,
shallowly breathing,
through the interminable, radiant white.

Dew parched mornings of brown grass
ascend to heavy shocked
saturate blasts,
until even birds won't feed
and mute shade their racing blood.

Then a fluke—a coolness—
a day or two of brilliant widest blue
the slanting golden light of promised fall,
pure fragrance of fresh water
waving from the earth and air.

Waiting

The breeze, stronger than usual,
rumpled leaves, turned them inside out,
caused them to resemble another genus.

Summer was old, hot, tired;
sun baked red clay was dust
that clung to banks of gravel roads.

A lone crow flushed from the brush
stirred the dust; flew away
in a cloud like shifted flour.

Only days before, the rain left
the world feeling like a fish tank,
underwater, with oppressing humidity.

The sun, shimmered through muggy air,
caused sweat to run into eyes,
drip upon glasses on down turned heads.

Then, the heat dried out the dampness;
the moisture less air blasted faces
as if a heated oven door was opened.

Fall, a welcome thought,
anticipated with pleasure, but now
the wait was intense, impatience mounting,
chafing for change, in all things hopeful.

The Mountains of the Tsalagiyi'

Tsalagiyi' (Cherokee people) pronounced *sal la ge ye*

Those Scot ancestors worked hard
for bare survival
along the rock strewn slopes,
carving out a place to make a life.

Discouraged offspring sought easier times
migrating to urban habitats
to make a living
that promised less difficulty.

Ease of living sustained less physical output
but wrought its price in anxiety,
in the stress of keeping up,
maintaining civility.

Routine hours and days, weekend warriors,
years that came and went
like uneasy dreams
over lost time.

Their blood runs in my veins;
calls out to me from the silent shadows
of green and brown
 as something gone astray.

I returned to the land of the Tsalagiyi'
that beckoned me over the years
to find the peace and solitude
of an unpretentious life.

The Anniversary

Memories graze the valleys of my mind
as the day wanders its way toward evening.
To ignore the sound, echoing in time,
of the song my heart once sang, is useless.

Silent pictures of moments frozen for eternity
float one on top of the other to the surface,
as awareness tries to avoid collision with them.

Morning acknowledged the span of time
with buffered recognition;
through the day, the reality of doing
repressed sharp awareness of the date.

As the day wore on, chinks of light sharpened
the shadowed retrospection, like shafts of lightning
bring clarity to dark corners.

Toward evening as the dusk closes in,
the silhouettes become clear against the pale sky.
No longer can the overpowering recollections
of day retreat to the safety of forgetfulness.

As a picture develops in the chemical wash,
so the memories materialize clear and sharp,
cutting deeply into consciousness.

Heavy with nostalgia, they lie hurting,
ruining the neatly constructed facade
that time and distance created,

sending waves of reminiscence against
the castles of sands of my mind.
Beautiful, sweet, recollections of another life
whose fulfillment lay in the ashes of dreams.

PAUL DONOVAN

Mustard Seed

We are one,
I know this,
I have always
known this.

Just as the
mustard seed,
the smallest of
all seeds,

sheds its shell
unfolding and growing
to the greatest
of all herbs,

so it is true
that all mankind
comes to perfection
bursting its self-limitations

and becomes
        one
with the
        One

At What Cost

There have been times
when I questioned
our love for each other.

Anger, words that hurt,
confusion, misunderstandings,
all a part of life.

Life becomes an art
of living
in this stressful world,
attempting to make sense
of it all.

We often find ourselves
trying to relieve
the pain of others
at the risk of
hurting each other.

Would our life, our
time together
be enhanced,
if we withdrew
within ourselves?

I believe, we enhance
who we are, seeing
the world through
loving eyes.

Glimpses

of majestic mountains
peeking through
low-lying clouds

of embracing beauty
surrounding us
wherever we go

glimpses

of soaring hawks
searching for
their morning prey

a red fox
scurrying through
protective woods

glimpses

of raging waters
crashing over
wet shining boulders

brave canoers
challenging fate
life on edge

glimpses

life going by
not involved
that's gonna change

just as soon
        as...

From the Window Seat

Diamond necklaces were strewn in circles.
Bracelets of topaz and emerald
brightened the ground in the black night.
We saw rings of all colors, one an arena.

Mom and I flew back in sunlight, watched
an onyx line snake for hundreds of miles,
light and dark, with specks and glints
of gold and silver, living beside its bulges and fingers.

Ridges to the north were topped with a brighter
white than the cloud puffs around us.
Below were swirls of jasper and agate
on squares of tans and browns.

Who made the gold and jade crop circles?
Stratus stretched to a long, pink curve.
We watched a rainbow ring on the wing
move with us, until the surrounding

heavens looked like a huge, gray pearl.
Far behind us ended the colorful West.
The sky turned azure and we zoomed
into autumn to greet the peak of Atlanta's colors.

After the Hail-Storm

I walked in my yard after
the hail-storm. Huge hostas
were sliced as if with a knife.
Boxwood's tiny leaves turned
brown on the ground.

Bombarded with scary news,
wretched and gory TV,
I dreamed of suicides
disguised as murders,
beheadings with swords and fire.

I must sooth my eyes and soul
with inspiring poems and stories,
so my mind can dream of those
who care and are rewarded with joy.

Giving

When January winds kept us inside,
Mom and I we attacked old maple chests.
There was sorting and giving to be done.

We put poetry books where there'd been
caps and coins, pens and medicine.
Soon there was an empty dresser.
I have a friend whose child needs it.

Someone who fishes will get a kick
out of these "trout" socks, still in the box.
The peace lilies that graced the church
went to homes with sunnier windows.

Dad's nurse came with milkshakes to share.
We gave him pie. Daddy ate key lime
the night before he died.
Key limes, the color of peridot.

How he loved to cut gemstones.
What's your wife's birthstone? I asked.
November, he said. *So was my Dad's.*
Will this ametrine do? It shines from gold

to purple. And for you a jasper bolo.
I looked at the many stones and rings,
remembering the times Dad showed me
his latest crafted treasure.

Mother

For all the safety and comfort
that you were not,
and for all the ways
I wish you knew
the woman I have become,
I still miss you
in the tears beneath my tears.

I miss you, this time of year.
Your sparkling eyes, hearty laugh,
your constant pride, your cakes, cookies,
and misplaced intentions
held me up when nothing else was there.

You endowed me with sewing,
colors that go together
and hope beyond hope.
Your obsessive optimism
tied our life together,
serged rough edges
into a decorative seam.

A thousand times I paced
my wooded path
the night before your death.
I heard the Banshee cry.
Your dying days became my relief.
I craved your approval.
Giving up spiraled my completion.

Midsummer Night

Evening light wells up
soft and tranquil,
the mystic creek flows forever
over frigid rocks.
A nightly symphony
of crickets and running water
begins when twilight matures.
Near the end of dusk
I dance with fireflies
as day is done.
A whippoorwill calls.
I go inside.

Tonight, near midnight
a loneliness wells up
inside the walls
and under the floor.
Emptiness prevails.
Birds don't sing.
Prayers seem unheard.
Only a book
can fill the void.

I wait for clarity,
conjure contentment
more than exuberance,
and I wait for morning.

Salvage

It was the lumber that called me
to the barn. Years and years of storage
blocked my way.

I found the plastic tubing we used for a level,
building the foundation of our house.
Back then it was clear, just like our life.
Now it's black from ages of disuse.

Fly-fishing line appeared, then our tent
that housed us along the trails of our youth.
A dibbling bag for planting and a shearing knife
to trim the Christmas tree crop showed up in one corner.
Six rusted hand saws hung on the wall,
along with drill bits, carving tools,
and a broken whetstone.
Once we were fervent in our farming chores.

Little boy clothes showed up,
and Teenage Mutant Ninja Turtles,
matchbox cars, and Legos.

I found my life, right where I left it,
before we let the woodshop go to hell,
before the barn became a storage shed.
I swept up dirt, leaves, nails and screws.

Now I clean up the cobwebs of my life.
I don't go near the crib we built
when I was pregnant. I ignore the bed
that used to be ours.
I will not look you up
to tell you what I've done today.

Pittsburgh 1960

crusty pie shell burnt black
cobblestone streets not yet chic
just hazards to tired old ladies

three rivers converging mixing it up
blending under the Point Bridge
too narrow for the cars that converge
like the rivers   now rivers of steel
where wheels argue with trolley tracks
that lacerate the road

Ft. Pitt tucked away gets little respect
not like the Liberty Bell
held by her proper cousin to the east
and old Forbes Field   chipped and scraped
good enough for the World Champion Pirates
the Cinderella team   perfect for such a city

and always steel mills
pure flames   smoke   grit
laying out carpets of grime
that cover the ledges   cover the city

Pink Lady Plays Golf

Glossed lips glisten under a straw hat
tied with a rose colored ribbon
on hair made right
by Mr. Michael every Thursday.
Frosted nails by Ingrid brush her
hot pink and green skirt.
She stands on the first tee,
flamingo on display,
personal golf cart,
a blushing chariot.
An 80 compression ball
sits like a pickled egg
on a powder pink tee.
She addresses the ball to perfection,
thanks to lessons by Chris.
Her score?
Three new party invitations
and a tete a tete at five.
Even par.

Traffic

If I could merge in traffic,
on an interstate, I would cut
the umbilical cord that ties me to others.

I would crawl out of a chrysalis
with wings no longer bound
but stretched unfurled,

travel anywhere without fear
of horns, collisions, or tying up a rush
hour road with 9-1-1.

I wouldn't take twice the time
to get somewhere
along a welcome two-lane road

with comfortable double lines,
no decisions, no need to apologize
to the line of cars that follow me.

I would travel two lane roads by choice,
and merge onto eight lanes
with in-your-face abandon.

ANN CAHILL

Saying Goodbye

A walk into the woods on a day bright with snow
still clinging to evergreen boughs
and deep enough to crunch underfoot,
deer gone wherever deer go when leaves are snowed
and the air is heavy with cold,
witch hazel branches black against a leaden sky,
red berries on a spiceberry bush, a Turner splotch
in the canvas of black and grey and white.

And all at once I remember
a forsythia hedge seen from my window, twigs black
where snow had slid away, and on the hedge,
in line, nineteen scarlet cardinals,
nineteen cardinals on black branches dotted with snow.
Nothing moved, not a whisper of wind, not a footfall,
not a feather, my breath indrawn softly
to make no sound, though nothing could have heard it
behind a pane of glass. The tableau was frozen
in time, the watcher not an intruder
but a participant in an unexpected
moment of grace.

First Frost

The dogwood outside the kitchen window
is red now. The birds have eaten the berries.

I lay awake last night
listening to the BBC
describing a world at the edge of fire,
and telling the hours,
three, four, God help me, five,
at six I slept. So this morning,
instead of feeding the cats at seven,
I lay under a tangle of comforters
until close to ten. Still in my nightgown
I stand by your chair. "Did you get anything
for breakfast?" You shrug your shoulders.
Do we have anywhere we have to go today?

"I do," I say, as I fill your cereal bowl.
"An ICL class at one, and chorus at six."
You read aloud a funny paragraph
in your Edmund Crispin novel. I laugh
as I had laughed at the same passage yesterday.
I sip coffee and read the *Times.*
Do we have to be anywhere today? "I do," I say,
"My poetry class at one, and chorus at six."
You finding anything interesting?
I show you Krugman's column. As always, we agree.

On the hill outside the window, the oaks are still green.
There will be time before they start their scarlet
progression, and more before the leaves brown
and fall. *Is there anywhere we have to be today?*
I kiss your forehead. "I do," I say.

Farm Pond with Geese

Two, then two more
a dozen, more than I can count
they fly in, blotting out the sun,
honking like Parisian taxis.
They settle on the pond
dark heads raised. I think
they know they are beautiful.
The effect of serenity is illusory.
There are too many; not every one
has its space on the pond. Late comers
crowd the banks, looking for open water.

Serenity is the farm house, seated
where it has been for generations.
The first settler chinked the logs for the home's beginning,
built a stone addition as the family prospered. His grandson
added again in wood, spacious, not too grand,
but fitting for a man of consequence.
Right to left: log, built against the weather,
doors that catch the head of the unwary;
stairstep up to stone, cool against summer's heat, and handsome,
fireplace in every room, warm October through March.
Another jog to the last addition, high-ceilinged, proud with paint.
Log, stone and wood, settled into the earth as if it grew there.

Zoom in on the postcard scene. The house, the pond
the overhanging trees, the geese flying in to settle.
Quickly zoom out again. Beauty is best seen from a distance.
It is not necessary to see the house beginning to sag,
the snapping turtle waiting for the goslings,
the banks where geese have left their mark—
you would not want to walk there.

Advance Directives

Most hope to die

in our sleep

owing no one

presence

no excuses

necessary

sparing

spared

cradled

in the grace

of dreams

saved

for last.

Fall

If I were to warn you
in a poem I could say
"There is a treachery
of ice beneath snowfall"
and you would comprehend
that all is not as it appears

but we are young
and we slip
for I have not begun to write
and you never learned
to read.

Ligatures

This is some craft:
with wit of silk
threads of recurrence to slip and knot
and man who learns
to reconstruct
as near he can
perfect scale, image, flesh
of one another,
to close exacting boundaries,

this thin line
drawing together
some sutured definition
of what holds us in
this life.

GENE HIRSCH

By the First Light of Day,

I see the outline of your face.
My eyes turn beyond,
to the strokes of black cedar
cast against an orange sky.

Boughs of the willow
bend in the breeze,
to the sheen water
that lies before them;
a breeze that wisps
your silver hair
from your eyes.

The rising sun streaks
across the pond
to glance your features,
splaying tiny opal hues
that kindle your smile.

I trace the furrows
in your face by the light
of the wakening day.
We love by the water's edge,
beyond the breeze,
beyond the strokes of cedar,
on the beautiful brink of the skyline.

Reaching for the Bottom of My Thoughts

My fingers waver,
knobbed and gnarled.
My pen lies near the telephone,
off its hook. I scrawl
across the umber pages
torn from old magazines,
my teacup, full.

I write letters. Pouring rain.
My cup is almost empty.
The telephone speaks
with a distant voice,
muffled, then mute.

I reach for the bottom
of my thoughts,
sipping the last drop,
summoning my love
whom I'd held
in my withered arms.

House

Cellos and fish,
musk for her nose
and small grains of cinders.

Shadow for her eyes.

A doll's hat
for a sea salt lunch
of bacon on a skillet
with flaking chips, wet
with talking ducks
in a nursery,

gone to the store
for a husband
with whom
she can play house.

CONTRIBUTORS

ANN CAHILL is a retired lawyer who lives in Blairsville, Georgia. She fell in love with the northeast Georgia mountains. She has studied with Nancy Simpson and Gene Hirsch. She belongs to Ridgeline Literary Alliance, North Carolina Writers Network West, and The Shallow End, a biweekly critique group.

PAUL DONOVAN lives in Murphy, North Carolina. He has been writing poetry since the early 1980s. His poems have appeared in anthologies, such as *Lights of the Mountains* (which he co-produced). He has published "Ramblings of an Idiot." He is a member of North Carolina Writers and North Carolina Writers Network West.

LUCY COLE GRATTON is a retired CPA living in Murphy, North Carolina. She has written poetry and prose for many years. Her interests include protecting our natural environment and her home on Lake Appalachia. She is a member of the North Carolina Writers Network and Ridgeline Literary Alliance. Her poetry has appeared in *Wild Goose Poetry Review* and *Skive Magazine.*

GENE HIRSCH is an academic geriatrician living in Pittsburgh, Pennsylvania, and Murphy, North Carolina. For fifty years, he has taught human values and the emotional care of sick and dying people to medical students and doctors. He has lectured widely. He teaches poetry at the John C. Campbell Folk School. His poems have appeared in many medical and non-medical journals as well as in books and anthologies. He is a member of the North Carolina Writers Network, Ridgeline Literary Alliance, and the Pittsburgh Poetry Exchange.

JOAN M. HOWARD lives in Hiawassee, Georgia, where she enjoys kayaking, birding, and boating on beautiful Lake Chatuge. She has been writing seriously for twenty years. Her poetry has appeared in *Lucid Rhythms, Our Pipe Dreams, The Deronda Review, The Road Not Taken: The Journal of Formal Poetry, Victorian Violet Press, The Aurorean, Wild Goose Poetry Review* and others. She is a member of North Carolina Writers Network, North Carolina Writers Network West, and the Georgia Poetry Society.

LINDA KANE has lived in the north Georgia mountains and has been writing for the past fifteen years. She draws on her life experiences as nurse and caregiver. Her poems have appeared in the *Lights in the Mountains* and *Freeing Jonah* anthologies.

MARY RICKETSON, Murphy, North Carolina, has been writing for twenty years. She is inspired by nature and her work as a mental health counselor. Her poems have appeared in *Wild Goose Poetry Review, FutureCycle, Journal of Kentucky,* and in her chapbook *I Hear the River Call My Name.* Anthologies include *Lights in the Mountains, Echoes Across the Blue Ridge,* and *Freeing Jonah.* She is a member of North Carolina Writers Network and Ridgeline Literary Alliance.

DIANA SMITH lives in Young Harris, Georgia and has been writing since she was a child reading Mother Goose. She has been published in *Main Street Rag, Asheville Poetry Review, Highlights, Hopscotch,* and the *Poets for Peace* and *Absolutely Angels* anthologies. She received Letters of Merit for poems from the Society of Children's Book Writers and Illustrators.

LINDA M. SMITH lives in Hayesville, North Carolina. She has written for many years. She has been inspired by the mountains. Her poems have appeared in ten anthologies including *Echoes Across The Blue Ridge* and *Freeing Jonah V.* She received awards for four poems in the county's annual Arts Council poetry contests. She is a member of the North Carolina Writers Network West (serving as coordinator of their readings at the John Campbell Folk School) and Ridgeline Literary Alliance.

Cover and interior book design by Diane Kistner; Gentium Book Basic text and Cronos Pro titling

ABOUT RIDGELINE LITERARY ALLIANCE

We are an alliance of writers and fans of writing in the mountain regions of the Southeast (western North Carolina, northern Georgia and South Carolina, and eastern Tennessee). This is our mission:

- To offer writers of all ages the opportunity to participate in and learn about the writing life

- To be a positive influence in education, promoting literature with talks and other suitable presentations in the classrooms of middle and high schools as well as in colleges and universities

- To proactively engage arts and cultural organizations by promoting literature in their communities and by attempting to heighten awareness and benefits of the literary arts

- To sponsor or participate in public literary events such as book festivals, readings, and workshops

- To explore avenues for publication, including online and in print, and to stay abreast of technological innovations in publishing

- To supplement and enhance the activities and services of other local literary organizations in the mountain regions

We seek to collaborate creatively and productively with other arts organizations in the area and beyond. We are incorporated as a non-profit in the state of North Carolina. Membership is free and open to anyone in the Southeast who is interested in being part of our work. For more information, please stop by our website:

www.ridgelineliterary.org

www.ingramcontent.com/pod-product-compliance
Lightning Source LLC
Chambersburg PA
CBHW032106040426
42449CB00007B/1210